Contents

The game of football   6

Mastering the ball   8

Kicking the ball   10

Dribbling the ball   12

Getting the ball   14

Goalkeeping   16

Heading the ball   18

Playing as a team   20

Fouls and free kicks   22

Corners and throw-ins   24

Small-sided games   26

Glossary   28

Further reading   29

Further information   29

Index   30

The game of football

Football is probably the most popular game in the world. It can be played nearly anywhere by almost anyone – all you need is a flat space and a ball.

Football is played on a grass pitch by two teams. Most senior teams have eleven players but you can play with smaller teams. The aim of the game is for each team to try and score goals.

A football match is divided into two halves of 45 minutes with a break of 15 minutes at half-time. Small-sided games are shorter. At the end of the match, the team with the most goals wins.

STARTING SPORT

Football

Rebecca Hunter

Photography by Chris Fairclough

W

FRANKLIN WATTS

Schools Library and Information Services

First published in 2006 by
Franklin Watts
338 Euston Road
London NW1 3BH

Franklin Watts Australia
Level 17/207 Kent Street
Sydney NSW 2000

© 2006 Franklin Watts

ISBN: 978 0 7496 6901 0

Dewey classification number: 796.334

A CIP catalogue record for this book is available
from the British Library.

Planning and production by Discovery Books Limited
Editor: Rebecca Hunter
Designer: Ian Winton
Photography: Chris Fairclough
Consultant: Jim Foulerton, sports journalist

The author, packager and publisher would like to thank the following
people for their participation in this book: the staff and pupils of Presteigne
County Primary School.

Printed in China

Franklin Watts is a division of Hachette Children's Books.

Equipment

Footballs are made of plastic or leather. Beginners start with a light, size 3 or 4 ball. Later a size 5 ball is used.

Football boots should support your feet firmly and feel comfortable. If you are playing indoors, your boots should have a non-slip sole. If you are playing on grass, studs on the bottom of your boots will stop you from slipping.

A football outfit is called a strip.

Players' strip

A shirt, which can be short- or long-sleeved depending on the weather.

A pair of shorts, which should be quite loose so they don't slow you down.

Socks

Boots with studs for grip

Shin pads, which are worn under the socks to protect your legs.

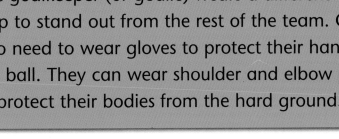

The goalie

The goalkeeper (or goalie) wears a different coloured strip to stand out from the rest of the team. Goalies also need to wear gloves to protect their hands from the ball. They can wear shoulder and elbow padding to protect their bodies from the hard ground.

Mastering the ball

Football is all about kicking a ball, so the most important skill to master is controlling the ball with both your feet. It is against the rules to use your hands, unless you are the goalkeeper.

Ball control

If you cannot control the ball, other players will take it from you. This exercise will help your ball control.

Start with your foot on top of the ball (**1**). Roll the ball to one side until your foot touches the ground (**2**). Then go back the other way until you touch the ground on the other side (**3**). Make sure your foot is in contact with the ball all the time. Practise this with both feet.

Juggling

You can juggle a football by trying to keep it in the air with your feet, legs, chest and head. Throw the ball in the air and then see how long you can keep it there without touching it with your hands or arms.

Juggling game

To play this game all players need a football and one player needs a whistle. All the players run with the ball until the whistle is blown. Then everyone flicks the ball up and juggles. The last one to keep the ball in the air is the winner. When he or she drops it, you all start again.

Kicking the ball

There are many different ways in which you can kick the ball. Each one uses a different part of the foot.

Inside of the foot

Using the inside of your foot is the easiest way to control the ball. Your

kicking foot should be at a right angle to your other foot. Kick the middle of the ball with the inside of your foot to make it go low and straight.

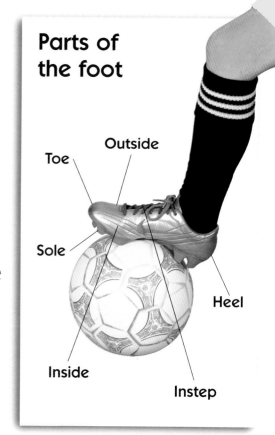

Parts of the foot

Toe

Outside

Sole

Heel

Inside

Instep

Instep

The instep is the part of your foot where your bootlaces are. Kicking the ball with your instep makes it go a long way. Take a long run up to the ball. Spread your arms out to the side to help you balance. Lean backwards and kick the lower part of the ball.

Trapping the ball

The first stage of passing the ball is getting it from a team mate. As the ball reaches you, move your foot back – this stops the ball bouncing away. Then hold, or trap, the ball under your foot. Trapping gives you control of the ball before you kick it again.

Two-touch game

In this game you may only touch the ball twice in a row. Trap the ball with the first touch, and then pass it with the second. If you touch it a third time you are out. You can also play this game by yourself against a wall.

Dribbling the ball

Dribbling is the skill of running along with the ball close to your feet, with you in total control of it. A good dribbler makes it seem as if the ball is tied to his of her bootlaces.

Learning to dribble

Push the ball a short way with the inside of your foot (**1**). Then straighten up the ball with the outside of your foot (**2**).

Repeat this over and over again until you feel you have complete control of the ball.

Now run forward as you do this (**3**). Remember to practise using both left and right feet for each move.

Dribbling drills

The best way to practise dribbling is to make an obstacle course. Dribble the ball in and out of the obstacles. Use the inside and outside of both feet to make the ball go different ways.

It is useful to know some clever tricks to get the ball past **opponents** who are trying to tackle you.

With a pretend pass (**1**), you pretend you are going to pass the ball to a team mate. Your opponent will move to intercept the pass.

Instead of making the pass, you run the other way (**2**). The opponent will be left in the wrong place and without the ball.

Getting the ball

Tackling is the skill of winning the ball away from the other team and keeping it. You must learn to tackle cleanly without tripping or kicking the other player or using your hands.

Marking and jockeying

A **marker**'s job is to stay close to an opponent to try to get the ball when it is passed to him. Jockeying is an important defending skill. It means getting in your opponent's way to slow him down. You need to keep about 1 metre away from him all the time.

Tackling

To tackle a player you should approach him from one side and try to get him to change direction. Put the inside of your foot against the centre of the ball just as he is about to pass it. If the ball gets stuck between your foot and your opponent's, try to flick it away. If you get the ball you must be ready to pass it to another player, dribble it up the field or shoot at the goal.

Tackling game

You will need four players, four balls and a marked-out square. Each player dribbles their ball within the square. At the same time you must try and kick the other players' balls out of the square. If your ball goes out, you are out of the game. The winner is the last player to keep his or her ball in the square.

Goalkeeping

The job of the goalkeeper is to stop the ball getting into the goal. If you are the goalie, you will need to be very quick, have good concentration and be good at catching and holding on to the ball.

The goalkeeper is the only player on the team who is allowed to use his hands. Gloves are worn to protect the hands and to make it easier to catch the ball.

Catching

To have a good chance of catching the ball, keep your hands close together with your fingers spread out. If the catch is from a high ball, keep your thumbs close together. If it is a low catch, keep your little fingers close.

High and low saves

To save a high ball you will need to jump. Push off on one leg only. This will help you to jump higher.

With a low shot, you must dive to save it. As the ball approaches, dive sideways with your arms outstretched. Your body and legs will form a barrier to help stop the ball.

Heading the ball

Sometimes the ball will be too high to kick. You are not allowed to use your hands but you can use your head. This is called heading the ball.

Warming up

Heading uses the muscles in your neck. You must warm up properly before trying to head the ball. First drop your chin forward and roll your head slowly from side to side.

Then hold your hand against the side of your head and push your head against it. Do this with each side of your head for a couple of minutes.

Basic heading

The most important thing to remember about heading is to go to the ball, not wait until it hits you! Stand with your feet apart to help you balance. Keep your eyes open and on the ball. Pull your head and body back and then move forward with force. Clench your neck muscles and meet the ball in the middle of your forehead. Try to aim the ball in the direction you want it to go.

Heading game

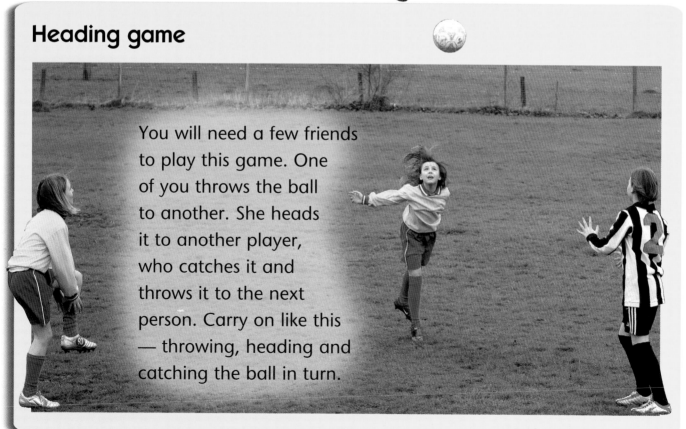

You will need a few friends to play this game. One of you throws the ball to another. She heads it to another player, who catches it and throws it to the next person. Carry on like this — throwing, heading and catching the ball in turn.

Playing as a team

To be a good football player you need to be a good team player. It is as important to help a team mate get or keep the ball as it is to get it yourself.

Apart from the goalkeeper, there are three types of position on the pitch. **Defenders** stay close to their own goal and try to stop the other team from scoring. **Attackers** stay closer to their opponents' goal and try to score goals. In between are players called **midfielders**. Midfielders help both attackers and defenders.

Formations

The number of players in each position is called the **formation**. The captain decides what formation to use. The most common formation is 4-4-2, meaning there are four defenders, four midfielders and two attackers.

Playing the game

Play starts with a kick-off. A coin is tossed to see which team kicks first. The **referee** puts the ball down in the middle of the pitch. A player kicks the ball to start the game.

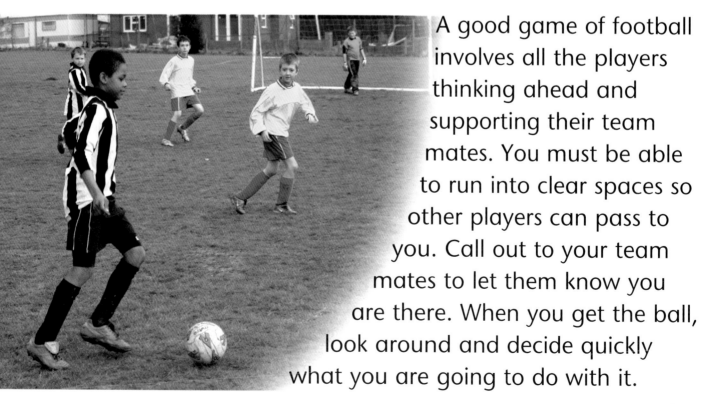

A good game of football involves all the players thinking ahead and supporting their team mates. You must be able to run into clear spaces so other players can pass to you. Call out to your team mates to let them know you are there. When you get the ball, look around and decide quickly what you are going to do with it.

Fouls and free kicks

Football has rules to make it safe and fair. Breaking a rule is called a **foul** and if you commit a foul the referee will give the ball to the other team for a **free kick**. There are two types of free kick: a direct free kick and an indirect free kick.

Direct free kicks

Direct free kicks are for serious fouls. These include kicking, pushing or tripping another player or touching the ball with your hands. A free kick is taken from the spot where the foul happened. Members of the other team have to be at least 9 metres away.

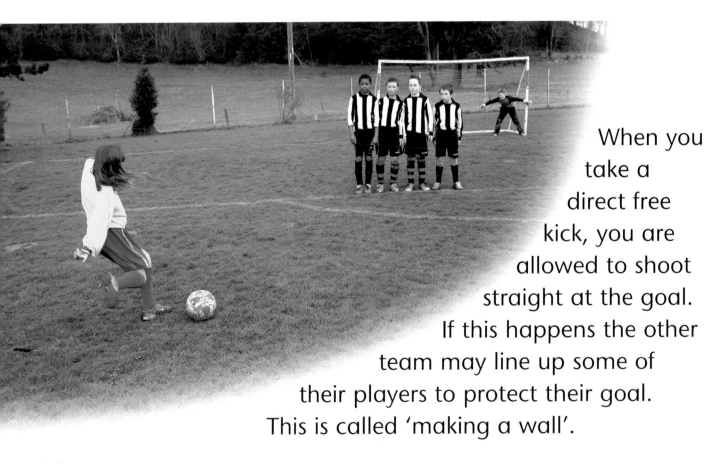

When you take a direct free kick, you are allowed to shoot straight at the goal. If this happens the other team may line up some of their players to protect their goal. This is called 'making a wall'.

Indirect free kicks

The referee may give an indirect free kick for less serious offences such as playing dangerously, obstructing the goalkeeper or charging a player who doesn't have the ball. If you are taking an indirect free kick you must pass the ball to another player before a goal can be scored.

Penalties

When a player commits a serious foul in his own penalty area, the referee awards the other team a **penalty kick**. A penalty kick is a shot at the goal from a place called the penalty spot. Only the goalie can try to stop the ball. The other players must stay out of the penalty area.

Goal line

Corner flag

Goal area

Penalty area

Corner circle

Penalty spot

Penalty arc

Touchline

Corners and throw-ins

During a game, if a team sends the ball out (over the lines at the edges of the pitch) the referee will stop the game and give the ball to the other team. How the game starts again depends on which line the ball crossed.

Corner kicks

If a player kicks the ball over their own goal line, the referee will award the other team a **corner kick**. You take a corner kick from the corner circle nearest to where the ball went out of play.

Goal kicks

If a player on the other team knocks the ball over your goal line (but it isn't a goal), the game is restarted with a **goal kick**. A goal kick must be taken from the goal area and it must leave the penalty area. Goal kicks are usually taken by the goalkeeper (right).

Throw-ins

If a team kicks the ball over either of the touchlines at the side of the pitch, the other team is allowed to throw it back onto the pitch. This is called a throw-in. This is the only time when a player – who is not the goalie – can use her hands. To take a throw-in you must stand just outside the touchline where the ball crossed the line.

Small-sided games

Football is normally played with eleven players on each team, but it is possible to have games with far fewer players. Small-sided games usually have five- or seven-a-side, but you can play with as few as three players.

Small-sided games are basically the same as eleven-a-side with a few differences.

The pitch

In small-sided games the pitch is smaller. Two of these pitches can fit onto one full-size pitch. Having a smaller pitch also means the game can be played indoors. The goals are smaller and there is a semi-circle instead of a box in front of each goal. Only the goalkeeper is allowed inside the goal area.

The game

Small-sided games are much shorter than real games. Each half may be only six or seven minutes long. The game starts with the referee dropping the ball between two players in the centre of the pitch. There is no kick-off. The game also restarts like this if the ball goes over the touchline.

The rules

The ball must not go above head height in small-sided games. If you kick it too high the other team gets an indirect free kick.

You can shoot at the goal from anywhere except inside the goal area.

Glossary

attacker a player who plays closer to their opponents' goal and tries to score goals.

corner kick a kick taken by the attacking side from the corner when the ball goes over the goal line but isn't a goal.

defender a player who plays closer to their own goal and tries to stop goals being scored.

formation the arrangement of the players on the pitch.

foul tripping, kicking or pushing an opponent; handling the ball.

free kick a kick awarded to a team that has been fouled by the opposite team.

goal kick a kick taken by the defending side when the ball goes over the goal line but isn't a goal.

marker someone who stays close to an opponent to stop them getting the ball.

midfielder a player who plays in the middle of the field.

opponent a player on the opposite team.

penalty kick a free kick awarded for a foul in the penalty area.

referee the official who controls the game and makes sure the players stick to the rules.

Further reading

Fantastic Football, Clive Gifford, Oxford University Press, 2006

Play Football, Catherine Saunders, Dorling Kindersley, 2006

I am a Striker: Talking About Football, Clive Gifford, Franklin Watts, 2006

I am a Defender: Talking About Football, Franklin Watts, 2006

Starting Soccer, Helen Edom & Mike Osborne, Usborne Publishing Ltd, 2004

The Everything Kids' Soccer Book, Deborah Crisfield, Adams Media Corporation, 2002

Further information

The Football Association
16 Lancaster Gate,
London
W2 3LW
Website: www.thefa.com

Football Federation Australia
26 College St
Sydney
NSW 200
Email: info@footballaustralia.com.au
Website: www.footballaustralia.com.au

Australian Sports Commission
PO Box 176
Belconnen ACT 2616
Australia
Email: club.development@ausport.gov.au
Website: www.ausport.gov.au

Index

attackers 20, 21

ball control 8, 9, 12, 13
ball size 7
boots 7

catching 16-17
corner kicks 24

defenders 20, 21
defending 14
dribbling 12, 13

foot parts 10
formation 21
fouls 22-23
free kicks 22-23, 24

gloves 7, 16
goalkeeper 7, 8, 16-17, 26
goalkeeping 16-17

goal kicks 24-25
goals 6, 22, 23, 24

heading 18-19

instep 10

jockeying 14
juggling 9

kicking 8, 10, 11, 21, 22, 23, 27
kick-off 21

marking 14
match 6, 21
midfielders 20, 21

penalties 23
pitch 6, 21, 23, 26
players 6, 7, 26
pretend pass 13

protective clothing 7

referee 21, 22, 23, 27

small-sided games 26-27
strip 7

tackling 14, 15
teams 6, 20-21, 26
teamwork 20-21
throw-ins 25
trapping 11

wall 22
warming-up 18